THIS STEP HOME:
SIMPLE GUIDE TO WALKING MEDITATION

JEFF FALCONER

Nowzville Books • Glen Ellen, California

This Step Home: Simple Guide to Walking Meditation
Copyright ©2017 Jeff Falconer

All rights reserved. No part of this book may be reproduced in any form, except brief excerpts for the purpose of review, without written permission from the copyright owner.

Nowzville Books
PO Box 1584, Glen Ellen, California 95442

ISBN: 978-0-692-90370-4

Cover logo: Gary Ruiz
Cover design: Nowzville Books
Book design: Novel Ninjutsu
Editing: Rebecca Lawton
Author photo: John Myers

www.jefffalconer.com

TO CLAUDE FALCONER

who woke me early to hike the hill and taught me:

Out with the bad air, in with the good air.

CONTENTS

Overlooking the Path	1
Focus	7
Breath	11
Body in Motion	17
The World around Us	22
Silence	33
Standing Meditation to Prepare	40
Attitude and Approach	49

IT IS SOLVED BY WALKING.

—St. Augustine

OVERLOOKING THE PATH

Walking Meditation has been practiced for centuries in many parts of the world and takes many forms. Some practices are strict and ritualized, others more free and easy. In my view, any activity that uses the simple and natural act of walking with a healing intent fits under the umbrella of Walking Meditation:

- Devotees of many religions undertake pilgrimages through holy lands in the footsteps of saints, seeking inspiration and closeness to God.

- Zen practitioners follow well-worn paths, counting their steps or repeating silent mantras, gaining clarity of mind and spirit.
- Many in the Western world enjoy labyrinth walking and attest to its powers in working through life's challenges and moving more in kinship with Spirit and Earth.
- Many Muslims circumambulate the Haj in Mecca as a required rite of passage, to be accomplished regardless of hardship or risk.

The Walking Meditation practice outlined in this little book may not be as dramatic or colorful as those just mentioned, but I have learned that heartfelt aspects of all of the above pursuits can be incorporated into an everyday regimen of Walking Meditation, bringing dramatic results.

The benefits of walking for exercise and recreation are well known and are excellent therapies for the body and mind: cardiovascular stimulation, deep breathing, gentle stretching, being outdoors, and exploring new areas.

Likewise the benefits of meditation are well known: increased clarity and focus, relaxation, an experience of peace and well-being . . . these all provide welcome respite in our busy lives.

Walking Meditation combines these benefits in an easy, natural activity that anyone can enjoy.

Many practitioners of Walking Meditation find that it offers a quicker path to the "payoffs" of meditation than sitting meditation, because the primal and kinetic act of walking is meditative in itself, and because the pressure-cooker experience that can accompany sitting still, alone with our thoughts and feelings, is lessened.

I practice both walking and sitting meditation almost every day, and I appreciate the unique gifts of each. Walking Meditation, though, is such an easy way to transform everyday tasks and events that I am quietly evangelical about sharing the gifts of the practice.

Cultivating a practice of Walking Meditation can enhance your experience of walking through the grocery store, walking the halls at work, or standing in line at the bank. On a daylong hike, or just a spin around the block, the inner clarity and harmony this simple discipline can bestow are very valuable and available to all.

Amid the hub-bub of modern life, full of multitasking and technologically driven urgencies, where most of us interact more with machines than we do with the natural world or each other, a practice of Walking Meditation can help us capture a precious autonomy, more fully inhabiting our bodies, our awareness, our moment in time, and our world.

The style of Walking Meditation presented here is non denominational. No new beliefs need be adopted, and no existing beliefs need be relinquished.

I hope you enjoy it.

FOCUS

Any meditation practice will involve an element of focus. One of the primary gifts of meditation is that it gives the thinking mind a rest and allows subtler aspects of the self to blossom. Thoughts so dominate our experience that it's helpful to give the mind a task to occupy it, a hamster-wheel to run around on, to give ourselves a moment's peace.

The object of focus can be a word, a sound, a candle, or the breath. In Walking Meditation my object of focus is simply the act of walking, and I approach this focus on three fronts: awareness of my breath; awareness of my body in motion, awareness of the world around me. Meditating on any one of these can provide a great experience, but I find that awareness of all three together gives full spectrum experience, involving all parts of myself.

Again, these three objects of focus are simply aspects of the greater act of walking; awareness of one will enhance awareness of the other. Relaxed awareness of breath will result in easier movement in my body overall. Feeling the life energy driving the breath will sharpen my eyes to the wonders of life in nature. Letting my arms, shoulders, and head move more freely as I walk will enhance the breath's range of motion, and so on. These inner connections create a cascading chain of benefits. There is intricate cooperation between all my systems that is inherent in the act of walking—mindfulness increases my appreciation and enjoyment of that very happy fact.

If you have difficulty maintaining full concentration, don't get too frustrated. You're not alone! As stated above, in our fast-paced, super sized world, our attention is constantly being pulled this way and that, all day every day. Exercising your power of concentration regularly is an excellent way to relieve information overload, and a great reminder that we aren't doomed to be scattered and stressed, blown forever like leaves in the wind.

BREATH

There is no more worthy focus during meditation than the breath, for a couple of reasons:

The breath is always with us, convenient and close at hand. If you find yourself without your breath at some point, you can stop worrying about what to meditate on.

The breath is our most tangible link to the wondrous energy of life. The same power compelling our lungs to pump, day in and day out, sleeping or awake, is animating every living thing on the Earth. Every blade of grass, every flower, every tree is sustained by this single life energy, as are all the fish, birds, animals, and humans on the planet. The energy of life is a force unimaginably vast and potent, but also possessed of intelligence that is intricate and surgically precise. Consider the humble seed, a tiny pulpy drop on the ground, programmed with the specific intelligence to grow into a rose bush, a corn stalk, or a redwood.

When we focus on and relax into the movement of the breath, we find ourselves resting on that very power, and in that very intelligence. Direct, conscious immersion in the power of life is nothing less than communing with our source, a nurturing experience like no other.

Relaxing into the breath, as opposed to simply watching it, lets us deepen and expand the breath's range of motion in the body. Most of us unconsciously "hold our breath," perhaps in reaction to life's stresses, repetitive occupations, habits of posture, or sitting for long periods every day. Relaxing into the breath's motion, we allow the breath to find its full, natural course. In both sitting and walking meditation, as we let ourselves go into the breath, and its range of motion increases, new spots of constriction present themselves to be unwound. Discovering and unwinding unseen tensions naturally prompt slight corrections in posture, creating, again, a cascading benefit to the whole body. This release of tensions can be a very pleasant experience.

When we walk, relaxing into the breath can reach optimal benefit. For example, while climbing a hill, notice how the breath will naturally speed up and deepen its course. If we consciously relax into this increased intensity, it can help to shake off held constriction, allow more oxygen into the lungs, and bestow a wonderful clarity of mind.

Continuous focus on the breath is the anchor of our Walking Meditation practice. With the mind thus occupied, we can observe the body in motion and our surroundings more purely, without interpretation. We can see, hear, smell, and feel without the running narrative of inner dialogue that most of us engage in without even noticing. From this quiet center, we can take experience simply as it comes to us. If a foot hurts, a foot hurts. If a hawk cries, a hawk cries. This purity of perception can be sublime.

A relaxed presence in the breath, as opposed to an obsessively intense focus, is to be cultivated. Strengthened power of concentration is a welcome by-product of keeping in touch with the breath in this way. Whether on a hike in the country, or on a busy city street, relaxing into the breath while walking cannot help but enhance our connection to the world and its deeper reality.

BODY IN MOTION

Awareness of our bodies in motion is a natural extension of relaxing into the breath. So often, we take for granted the innate abilities and cooperating systems of these amazing biological machines we inhabit. Walking Meditation can refresh our respect and appreciation for our bodies and our place in the natural world.

Start with feeling your feet on the ground. This is a most primal human connection. Feeling your feet on the earth, the sidewalk, or the carpet as you walk acts as a crucial root in your sense of place.

Hear the sound of one foot after the other touching down. Feel the texture of whatever surface you are walking on. Feel the smooth inner working of the feet as they transfer your body's weight from heel to toe, moving you forward. Feel the gentle action of toes gripping the ground.

Keeping your awareness centered in the breath, observe the gentle spiraling motion of the body as your legs and arms work in harmonic opposition, propelling you along. The pumping of the legs initiates the swing of the arms, the rocking of the shoulders, a gentle nodding tilt of the head, and a twist of the spine. Relax into all of this as one ongoing motion.

Know the innate intelligence of your body as it encounters changes in its path. Appreciate that obstacles such as rocks or roots on a country trail, or cracks and holes in an urban sidewalk, are negotiated largely without conscious thought.

Note how, in walking uphill, your body automatically leans forward, bringing itself to an upright "plumb" position, and how when going downhill, your body makes the opposite adjustment.

Feel the exaggerated swing of your arms in the effort to climb, along with the deepening and quickening of breath. This action also takes place without you having to think about it.

When walking on a crowded city sidewalk, or through the aisles of a store, appreciate how many small adjustments your body makes intuitively, in addition to the many other adjustments your body and mind make together. Speeding up, slowing down, moving side to side, stopping to wait—it's astonishing to observe and learn to respect the constant subtle interplay of our bodies and body-minds as we devote our mental energy to thinking about what we'll have for lunch or reliving the conversation we just had with a friend. As we'll see again and again, the practice of Walking Meditation is largely about appreciating anew what has always been.

THE WORLD AROUND US

Walking Meditation can be practiced anywhere, in a single room or on a busy avenue, in an office or on a mountain trail. The benefit of the practice is not dependent upon your surroundings, but the flavor of your experience can be nurtured in different and interesting ways by the immediate environment.

Walking mindfully in nature is, of course, wonderful. Being in intimate contact with the life energy within heightens sensitivity to its manifestation around us. With the understanding that one energy enlivens every blade of grass, every tree, and every creature that flies, swims, or creeps, walking through a dense forest can be powerful.

In nature we experience deeper kinship and connection to all life. Coming upon a field of wildflowers and taking in the riot of colors, the delicate individuation of one species from another, and the soft stubborn tenacity they embody, can be a revelation. Walking beside water, be it the ocean, a lake, or a stream, can provide a meditative enhancement all its own: appreciating the way water flows easily and naturally, taking the course of least resistance; hearing the sound of the stream's gurgle or the ocean's roar; smelling the refreshing scent of water and experiencing the soothing, familiar feeling that being near it imparts. Walking in the desert, surrounded by its stark testimony to the tenacity of life, can be wonderfully humbling. Being in nature heals and calms us because we are a part of it. The energy that the natural world embodies and exudes can feed us to the core. We belong to nature and it to us. It is home.

In urban settings, our connection with nature is not diminished, though it may not be so readily apparent. The earth is still the earth. The sky is still the sky. We still need the air we breathe, the water we drink, the food we eat, the sun that warms us, and the energy of life. In every city, wild animals still find ways to exist, to the frustration of their human counterparts. The sharp-eyed walker can spot hawks flying from high-rise perches, migratory birds and butterflies occupying parks, raccoons trundling to their tasks at night, and pigeons and squirrels staying busy all day. Likewise, in the urban jungle, the variety of human inhabitants is often accompanied by intensified displays in plumage and behavior. As we walk city streets, our kinship with nature in all living things can be fed in unexpected and amusing ways.

Appreciating the strictly human-made environment while walking through a city or town is valuable as well.

Negotiating the terrain of streets and alleys, bridges, and stairways, we feel their distinct texture and rhythm. Awareness of sound, in horns, vehicle noise, and voices can become as important a part of the meditative experience as hearing birdsong or a burbling stream in the woods.

Walking inside of buildings is still walking, of course, and so can be of meditative value. The muted sounds of human activity, with people instinctively speaking more quietly while working in cubicles and offices, the hum of technology, the sounds of a building's elevators and air systems, the texture of finished flooring or carpet underfoot, may not seem as alluring as a trail on a bluff over the sea, but the calm and clarity of meditation are still available.

Awareness of the environment we're in, as opposed to pining for the environment we wish we were in, is crucial in a mindful life. Understanding why we find ourselves where we are is important in the larger texture of human experience.

While Walking Meditation is not about encouraging excess mental activity, appreciating the human skill, planning, and ingenuity that went into creating the urban environment can also be nurturing and positive, if only in encouraging us to use our talents ever more wisely.

With my attention consumed in the breath and my body in motion, I can open my senses to my surroundings without the interpretation of my habitual inner narrative. I can let the green of the forest flood my eyes with soothing color and allow the sounds of birdsong to tickle my ears. I can perceive human-made structures of concrete, steel, and glass in all their massive solidity and open my ears to the hissing tires, shouting voices, and honking horns of the city.

Relinquishing my running dialogue, with its compulsion to name and explain, requires its own leap of faith. There is always a fleeting hiccup of panic when letting go of my precious opinions and perspectives, but the reward for this subtle surrender is being more fully present. Everything that my senses present me with while walking mindfully is totally in the moment, the sights and sounds of now. I am in my most vital and animal self, a living, breathing primate moving through my world. The momentary vulnerability I feel when I first let go of my dialogue is soon replaced with a wonderful aliveness, and an innate knowledge that I am actually more in tune, more ready to react, more fully touching and being touched by my environment than at any other time.

In this eternal moment, I often have the liberating realization that "I" am simply a point of awareness in the center of all this matter and motion. My breath is generated by the larger power of life. My body is composed of elements from the earth, to which it shall return. The world around me existed when I arrived in it, and will still be humming along when I leave. This may seem morbid to some or fanciful to others, but it is certainly part of the texture of my life. I value such vivid moments of clarity, which are both humbling and inspirational.

When the mind wanders from meditation, as it surely will, simply bring it gently back into focus. It makes no difference how far or how long the attention has strayed, or whether the mind is ruminating on world conquest or a snack. An often-used analogy is treating the mind like a small child whose attention has wandered from a chore or a game. Recriminations, lectures, or agonizing over underlying causes would be out of proportion with the severity of the lapse, as well as a waste of time and energy. Just direct the mind gently and lovingly back to the breath, body in motion and surroundings.

SILENCE

Try to practice Walking Meditation in silence. It is entirely possible to be mindful and hold a conversation, of course, but abstaining from talking enhances the ability to listen and look without distraction and to more fully enjoy breath and body in motion. It is all too easy to get lost in conversation, just as it is in thinking. The experience of meditation goes much deeper with undivided attention on the act of meditation. A continuity of awareness is key here.

We spend so much time relating to words and thoughts that simply "giving it a rest" from time to time is helpful in keeping a healthy overview. People in our era are clearly obsessed with labels, identification with ideologies, and promoting and defending cherished beliefs of what is right or wrong. It's important to keep an eye on issues of concern, and to feel passionate about what is right in our view, but that is not all there is to life, not by a long shot. Our current gossip culture, awash in cruel snark, fraught with trivial concerns, and driven by media bent on convincing us to buy products we don't actually need with money we may not actually have, is a stark example of the downward spiral that individual minds and group mind are capable of. It is all too easy to be led into believing that what we think and what we hear spoken around us represents reality. Words and thoughts certainly represent one stratum of our reality, but not the whole of it, and not the most satisfying portion by far.

Walking mindfully in silence brings you back to the immediate reality of you, in your body, in your moment, in your world. The absolutes at this level of experience are not negotiable or open to interpretation. If the day is hot, if your beginning mood is foul, if the trail is steep—these are the actual textures of the moment you are working with. Relaxing into the simple movement of the breath, watch the influence of those conditions begin to dissolve into the background. Feeling the gentle massage of your body in motion, feel a little of the pleasure of being alive creep back into your awareness. Enjoy the feeling of your energy expanding, getting bigger, touching and being touched by your surroundings. Letting your awareness see and hear and smell the physical world around you, with the solid earth beneath your feet and the open sky above, watch your worries step back for a moment. "Taking a breather" in this way will not make you uncaring or disconnected. It will make you more effective, by clearing and uncluttering your perceptions, softening your heart, and reaffirming your oneness with your living world.

In cultivating a silent practice, a little goes a long way, so for starters, short periods of silent walking can be very beneficial. If you have walking partners, as I do, with whom you habitually converse while hiking, perhaps suggest a few moments in silence to expand and enhance the pleasure of the walk. Five minutes will seem like a long time, if you're not accustomed to this discipline, but five minutes of silent walking can work wonders.

As stated, I have hiking buddies with whom I have a tradition of discussing "the state of the universe" in most esoteric and uncensored terms. I still enjoy that thoroughly and wouldn't trade it for a million bucks. But even when we're topping the hill yammering about an old *noir* film or a new conspiracy theory, my walking meditation practice often sneaks in out of habit. When that happens I benefit on multiple levels. I love that.

STANDING MEDITATION TO PREPARE

If I have a moment before I begin my walk, I like to start with this standing meditation, which I have cobbled together from my happy explorations in Qigong and Tai Chi. An abbreviated version is fine, if that's all time allows. The idea is simply to begin to be aware of the points of focus I'll be working with while walking. This standing meditation can be done with eyes closed or open, but the attention should be turned within, in either case.

Stand with feet roughly shoulder width apart. Bend your knees slightly, not going into a crouch, but unlocking and relaxing your stance. This posture will straighten the spine, ease tension in the upper body, and enhance a freer flow of breath. In the beginning and throughout the meditation, adjust your posture to find your most relaxed and effortless standing position.

Focus attention on the breath. Hear the sound it makes coming in through your nostrils, into your throat, and into your head and chest. Gradually let go into the movement of your breath, noticing and then relaxing into points in the body where you may be holding energy or making unnecessary effort. Begin to sink into your "natural breath" and enjoy its fuller range of motion. Pay attention to the moments of stillness at the top of the in-breath and the bottom of the out-breath. Feel the slight tickle of urgency as your body is prompted into the next inhale or exhale. That's the life force talking to you. Rest in this awareness for several breaths.

Maintaining focus on the sound and movement of the breath, bring your attention down to your feet. Feel the point of contact between your feet and the earth. Feel the weight of your body resting on your feet, on the earth. Relax there a moment.

Breathe your attention up through your ankles, calves, and shins, into the intricate skeletal structure of the lower legs, into your knees. Send a smile of appreciation to your knees for the part they play in your mobility and the genius of their design. Check to make sure they're still slightly bent. Feel the weight of your body resting on your knees, your feet, and the earth.

Breathe your attention up through the big bones and muscles of your upper legs: your thighs and quads. Appreciate the strength and power this part of your body brings to the act of walking. Take your time in breathing your attention into the hips. The word "hips" here refers to that entire, very important zone in the body's structure: hips, pelvis, sacrum; muscles of the butt; and pelvic belt. Appreciate the wondrous design of this part of your anatomy as well and the absolutely crucial function it plays as the nexus of power in your ability to ambulate, the very junction of function. Feel the weight of your upper body resting on your hips, your knees, your feet, the earth.

Now, breathe your attention up your spine, surrounded by the internal organs, your ribcage, your heart and lungs, the big muscles of chest and back. Truly the engine-house of biological function, your upper body deserves a special moment of appreciation and love. Enjoy the increased sense of aliveness your attention bestows, as you bring it slowly up into your shoulders. Again, "shoulders" here refers to that entire part of your structure: collar bones, shoulder blades, more big muscles, more genius design. Feel down your arms, all the way into your hands hanging relaxed by your sides. Feel the weight of your neck and head on your shoulders, on your hips, on your knees, on your feet, on the earth.

Breathe your attention up into the structure of your neck, jaws, and skull, into the muscles of your throat and face, into your eyes, ears, nose, and brain. This is the home of sense and speech, thought and judgment, the nerve center of the whole operation. The myriad functions that happen in this part of the body may defy our comprehension, but give it a nod anyway and rest a while in the appreciation of all the gifts of awareness and mobility in your most wondrous body.

Now feel the fullness of the body's awareness sinking downward into the earth but also reaching upward into the sky. This is not visualization. It is our right place on the line between heaven and earth. Let the top of your head feel the lightness and openness that concentration can bring, at the same time you feel your feet rooted in the earth. Rest here as long as you can.

Now open your eyes or raise your gaze to survey your surroundings. Feel the pleasure of seeing and hearing without the interpretation or inner dialogue. Keep attention on the breath and maintain the feeling of sinking into the earth. Enjoy the more complete appreciation of your body this meditation has hopefully granted.

And now, take a step.

ATTITUDE AND APPROACH

Walking meditation should be fun, pleasurable, and life enhancing. Too often in pursuits that may come under the heading of "spirituality," a certain solemnity and intensity of purpose can kick in. This is quite common, and generally counter-productive, in my experience. We're talking about taking a walk here! Moving, breathing, seeing, hearing, digging our world . . . these are wonderful gifts of human existence, so let's lighten up!

There is a wonderful essay by Thoreau called "On Walking," in which he discusses walking in Nature. He focuses much attention on the word "sauntering," coming fairly close to the point of saying, "If you're not *sauntering*, you're not *doing* it right!" I love that, because to me the image of sauntering through nature is one of looseness, a no hurry/no worry attitude, luxuriating in my world and myself. Sauntering expresses an attitude of confidence and belonging, as in, "Hey, man, I own this place!" Such an attitude is not mere arrogance. I do own this place, and this place owns me.

As stated before, the benefits of this practice are available on both short and long walks, but every once in awhile, given opportunity and ability, set aside time for a nice long jaunt. Whether in town or in the country, the rewards of an extended mindful trek, with a sustained period of concentration and easy breathing, can be dramatic. When I do get a chance to spend hours hiking for miles on my beloved local mountain, I get home feeling like my mind and spirit have been steam cleaned! It really is a beautiful feeling.

Any walk is a journey into the unknown, just as waking up every day is. The choice to explore is more about curiosity than courage. Human life is temporal and tenuous, with beginnings and endings and much uncertainty.

Fortune is fickle, so while I have the facility and opportunity to enjoy my body, my time, and my world, should I not do so?

When I practice Walking Meditation, I feel in touch with both my mortal and eternal qualities. I feel kinship with the heartbreakingly fragile and immovably solid aspects of both the natural world and the human one. I experience blessed stillness in the center of my movement. I am, for a moment, at peace on my journey.

For that, I'm profoundly thankful.

OTHER BOOKS BY JEFF FALCONER

This Timeless Breath:
Simple Guide to Sitting Meditation

Nowzville Books • Glen Ellen, California

www.ingramcontent.com/pod-product-compliance
Lightning Source LLC
Chambersburg PA
CBHW072113290426
44110CB00014B/1901